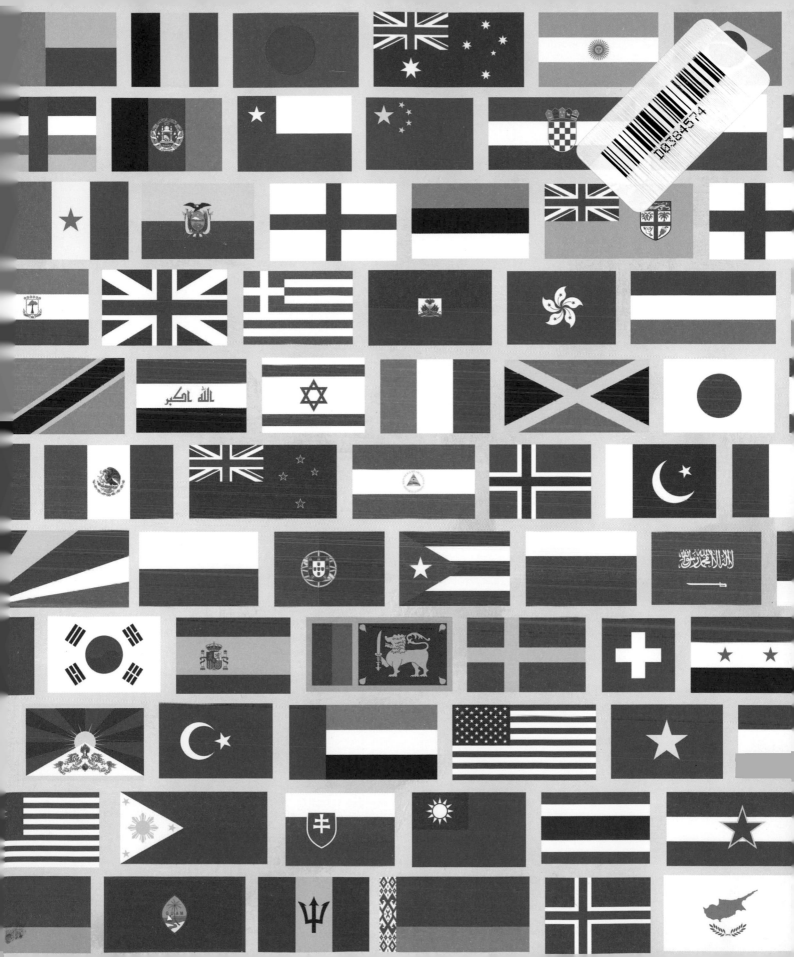

WHEN I GET OLDER
The Story Behind "Wavin' Flag"

K'NAAN

With Sol Guy

Illustrated by Rudy Gutierrez

TUNDRA BOOKS

Published in Canada by Tundra Books, a division of Random House of Canada Limited
One Toronto Street, Suite 300, Toronto, Ontario M5C 2V6

Published in the United States by Tundra Books of Northern New York
P.O. Box 1030, Plattsburgh, New York 12901

Library of Congress Control Number: 2011923472

Library and Archives Canada Cataloguing in Publication

K'naan

    When I get older : the story behind Wavin' flag / by K'naan with Sol Guy.

Includes lyrics of the song Wavin' flag.
ISBN 978-1-77049-302-5 (bound)

    1. K'naan – Juvenile literature. 2. Rap musicians – Biography – Juvenile literature.
3. Somali Canadians – Biography – Juvenile literature. 4. Somalia – History – Juvenile literature.
I. Guy, Sol II. Title.

ML3930.K675W56 2012   j782.421649092   C2011-901446-7

We acknowledge the financial support of the Government of Canada through the Book Publishing
Industry Development Program (BPIDP) and that of the Government of Ontario through the Ontario
Media Development Corporation's Ontario Book Initiative.

We further acknowledge the support of the Canada Council for the Arts and the Ontario Arts Council for our publishing program.

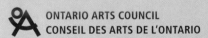

ONTARIO ARTS COUNCIL
CONSEIL DES ARTS DE L'ONTARIO

www.tundrabooks.com

Printed and bound in China

2 3 4 5 6   18 17 16 15 14

For Salaam and Talib –K'naan

For Sandflower, Elaine, Gregory Joseph, Shelley, Daniel G., LC, TS, Malcolm and Jordan.
"Always remember that you are beautiful and full of light
even when it seems dark, and always remember your way home." –R.G.

My name is K'naan. Until I was thirteen years old, I lived in Mogadishu, a city that was like a sparkling jewel. Mogadishu is in Somalia and sits on the Horn of Africa.

The entire Indian Ocean was my backyard. Boats came and went all day long, bobbing on sky-blue water.

I lived with my mother, my brother and sister, and my grandfather in a bright white stone house in the center of the busy city.

My grandfather was one of the most famous poets in all of Somalia. Whenever I didn't feel well, he would recite his poems to me as we watched the sun set. His poems were like medicine. They told the best stories I ever heard.

We didn't have a lot of money, so we often made our own toys. We made skateboards out of old wheels and pieces of wood.

One day, my friends and I rode our skateboards while holding onto a truck. We were afraid to let go, and the truck took us far away. We got in big trouble, but my mother never stayed mad for long.

One morning, I woke up to a scary sound like angry bees coming from the street outside my window. There was gunfire everywhere. Was this what war sounded like? We couldn't play outside anymore. Everyone was frightened.

My grandfather wrote me a short poem, and we read
it aloud together:

"When I get older, I will be stronger.
They'll call me freedom, just like a waving flag."

My mother wanted us to leave Somalia and
move somewhere safer. Every day, she walked to the
government buildings to try to get us the official papers
we needed to allow us to live in a new country.

I was frightened when she went out into the street,
but my mother was brave.

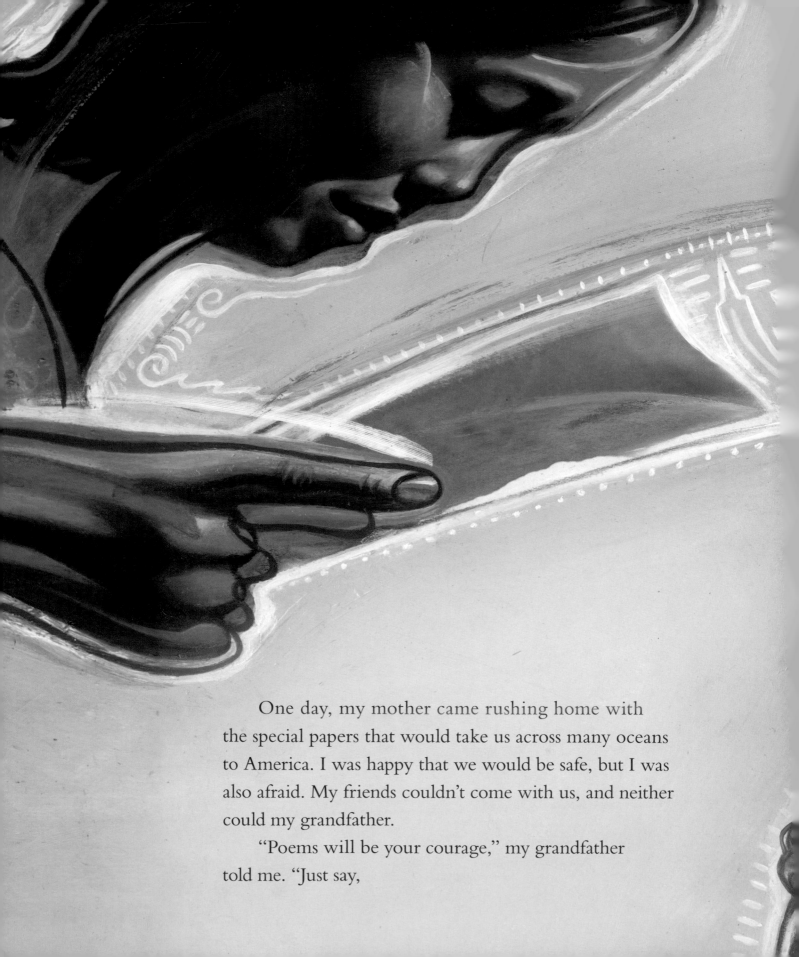

One day, my mother came rushing home with the special papers that would take us across many oceans to America. I was happy that we would be safe, but I was also afraid. My friends couldn't come with us, and neither could my grandfather.

"Poems will be your courage," my grandfather told me. "Just say,

'When I get older,
   I will be stronger.
 They'll call me freedom,
    just like a waving flag.'"

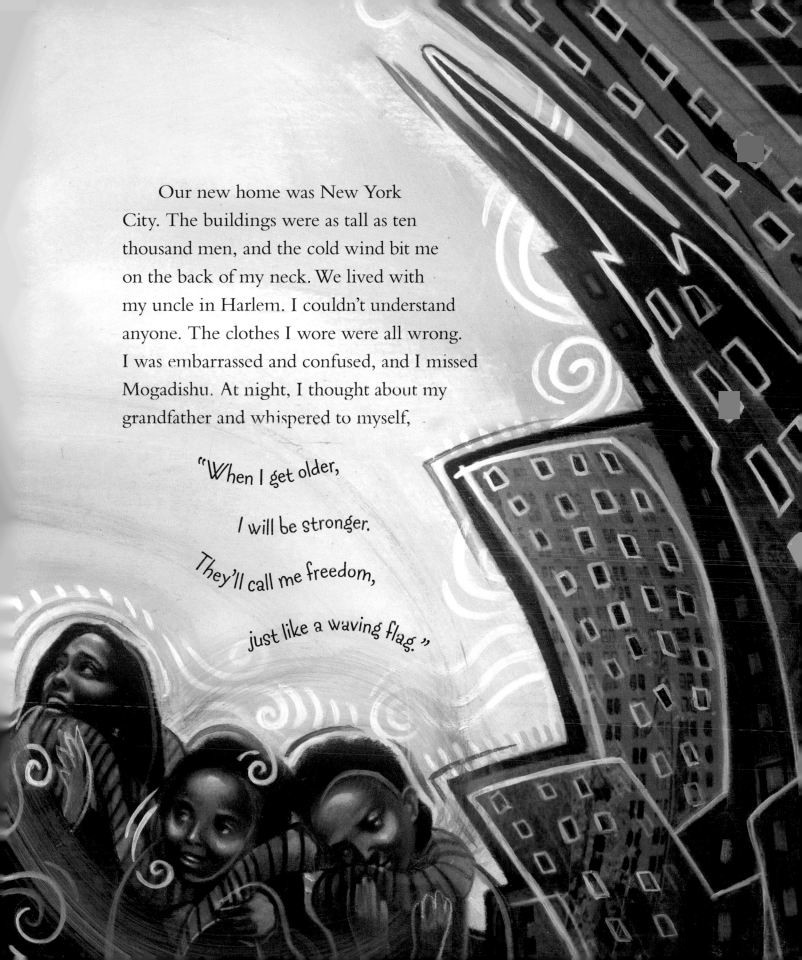

Our new home was New York
City. The buildings were as tall as ten
thousand men, and the cold wind bit me
on the back of my neck. We lived with
my uncle in Harlem. I couldn't understand
anyone. The clothes I wore were all wrong.
I was embarrassed and confused, and I missed
Mogadishu. At night, I thought about my
grandfather and whispered to myself,

"When I get older,

I will be stronger.

They'll call me freedom,

just like a waving flag."

When you come to a new country you need a lot of papers. We didn't have the right ones to stay in the United States, so after six months we had to leave again, this time for a place called Toronto, in Canada.

Canada gave us new papers and a new name: refugees. I didn't know what that meant. My mother said it was a name for people who had to leave a country because it wasn't safe. Canada was calm, and it felt safe.

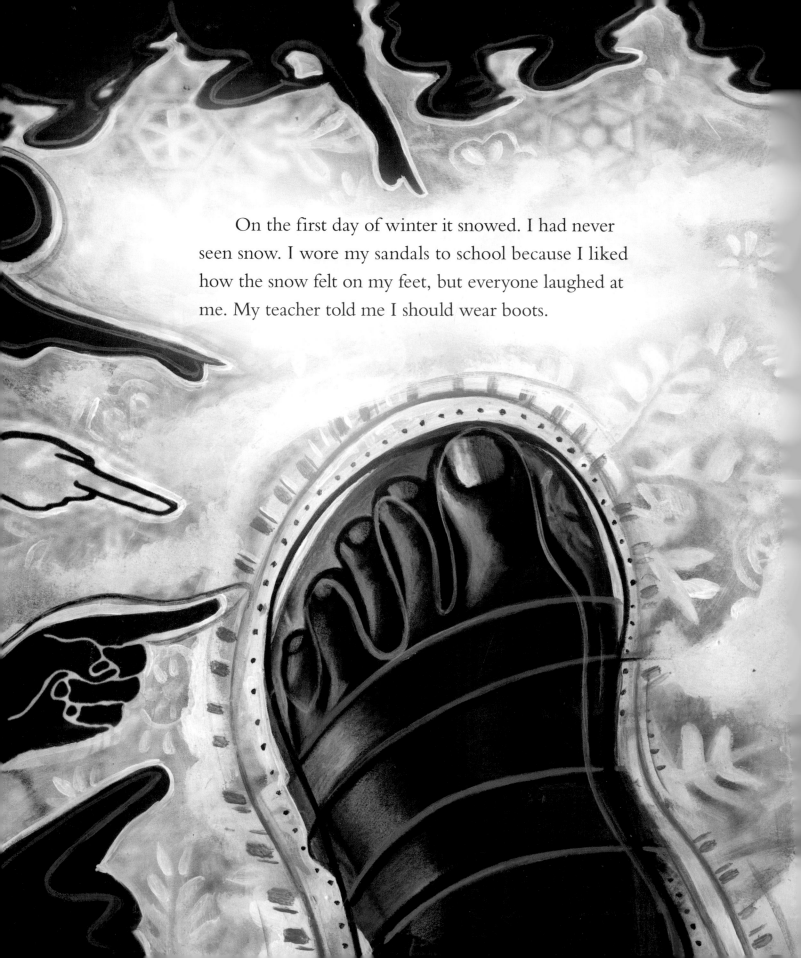

On the first day of winter it snowed. I had never seen snow. I wore my sandals to school because I liked how the snow felt on my feet, but everyone laughed at me. My teacher told me I should wear boots.

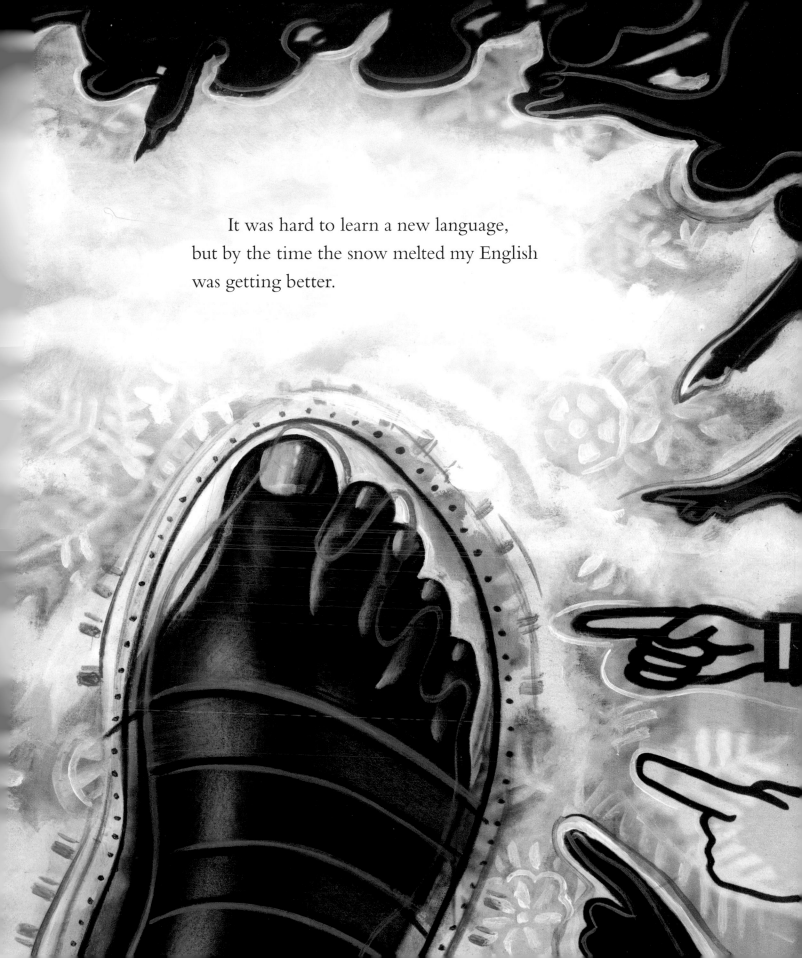

It was hard to learn a new language,
but by the time the snow melted my English
was getting better.

A boy called me a mean name and said Africa was dirty
and ugly. I got really mad, and I punched him. My mother had
to come to the school and talk to the teacher.

Mom told me I should talk about my feelings instead of
fighting, but this isn't always easy to do. Talking is better than
fighting – but singing is even better.

There were other kids at school who had to leave
a home far away and who struggled to learn a new
language. We all looked different, but we all liked
to play and we loved our music class, where
we got to sing. Songs are like poetry.

I told my new friends about my grandfather and the poem he wrote for me. They told me I was a good singer. Singing made me feel as if anything were possible.

"When I get older,
I will be stronger.
They'll call me freedom,
just like a waving flag."

At the end of the
school year, the teacher
announced that we had to sing
a song in front of the entire school.
I asked my friends from different countries
and my friends from Canada if they wanted
to sing my grandfather's poem with me.
I wasn't afraid anymore. Grandfather was
right. Music made me safe.

Wavin' Flag

Words and Music by
Keinan Warsame, Philip Lawrence, Bruno Mars, Jean Daval, Edward Dunne, and Andrew Bloch

Wavin' Flag – Lyrics

When I get older, I will be stronger,
They'll call me freedom, just like a wavin' flag.

When I get older, I will be stronger,
They'll call me freedom just like a wavin' flag.
And then it goes back, and then it goes back,
And then it goes, back, oh.

Born to a throne, stronger than Rome,
But vi'lent prone, poor people zone.
But it's my home, all I have known,
Where I got grown, streets we would roam.

Out of the darkness, I came the farthest,
Among the hardest, survival.
Learn from these streets, it can be bleak,
Accept no defeat, surrender retreat.

So we strugglin', fightin' to eat,
And we wonderin', when we'll be free.
So we patiently wait, for that fateful day,
It's now far away, but for now we say.

When I get older, I will be stronger,
They'll call me freedom, just like a wavin' flag.
And then it goes back, and then it goes back,
And then it goes back, oh.

So many wars, settlin' scores,
Bringin' us promises leavin' us poor.
I heard them say, "love is the way,
Love is the answer," that's what they say.

But look how they treat us, make us believers,
We fight their battles, then they deceive us.
Try to control us, they couldn't hold us,
'Cause we just move forward like buffalo soldiers.

But we strugglin', fightin' to eat
And we wonderin', when we'll be free.
So we patiently wait, for that fateful day,
It's not far away, but for now we say.

When I get older, I will be stronger,
They'll call me freedom, just like a wavin' flag.
And then it goes back, and then it goes back,
And then it goes back, and then it goes.

When I get older, I will be stronger,
They'll call me freedom, just like a wavin' flag.
And then it goes back, and then it goes back,
And then it goes back, and then it goes,
And then it goes.

And ev'rybody go, singing it.
And you and I will be singing it.
And we all will be singing it.

When I get older, I will be stronger,
They'll call me freedom, just like a wavin' flag.
And then it goes back, and then it goes back,
And then it goes back, and then it goes.

When I get older, I will be stronger,
They'll call me freedom, just like a wavin' flag.
And then it goes back, and then it goes back,
And then it goes back, oh.

When I get older, when I get older,
I will get stronger, just like a wavin' flag,
Just like a wavin' flag, just like a wavin' flag,
Flag, flag, just like a wavin' flag.

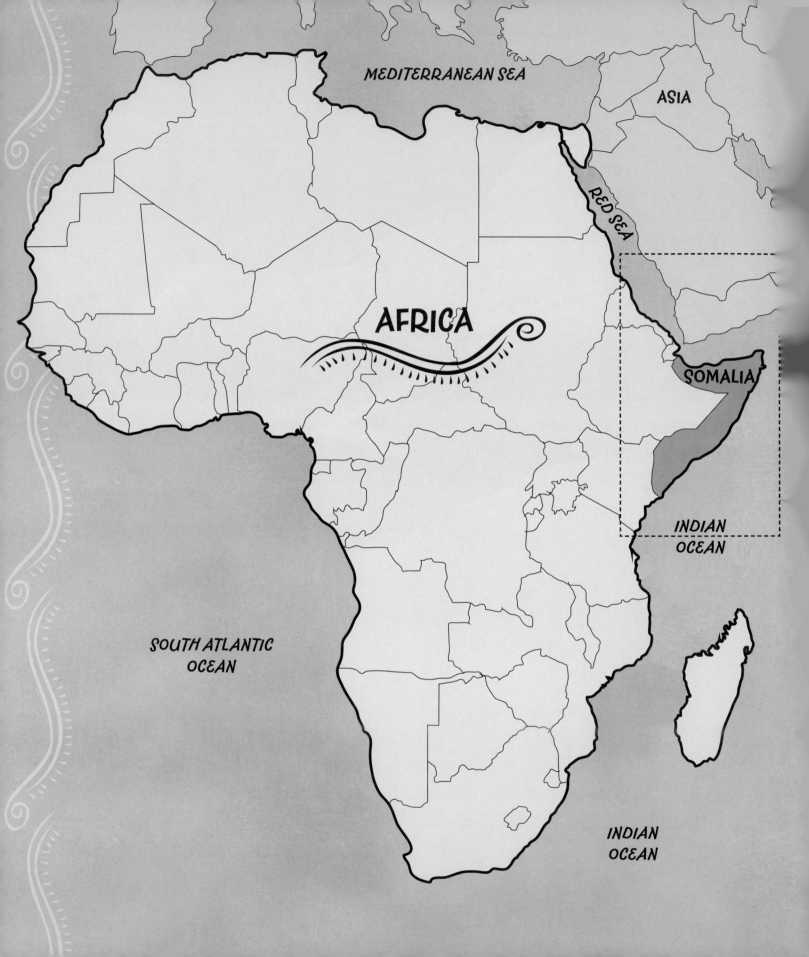

MEDITERRANEAN SEA

ASIA

RED SEA

AFRICA

SOMALIA

SOUTH ATLANTIC
OCEAN

INDIAN
OCEAN

INDIAN
OCEAN

A Brief History of Somalia

The **Republic of Somalia** is located on the Horn of Africa. The Indian Ocean is on the east side of the country, and Ethiopia and Kenya are on the west.

In ancient times, Somalia was an important trading post. It was a major source of spices and other luxuries, which were valuable to the Ancient Egyptians.

Over the centuries, Somalia has been ruled by different countries. In the late 1800s, northern Somalia became a protectorate of Britain, while the southern parts of the country were controlled by Italy. In 1960, the northern and southern parts of the country were united and became the Somali Democratic Republic. Somalia was one of the founding countries of the Organisation of African Unity (now the African Union) and supported the anti-apartheid movement in South Africa.

In 1991, the Somali Civil War broke out, and the government collapsed. The country has been in a state of war ever since. The situation has been made worse by drought and famine: many Somalis rely on agriculture for their livelihood, and most of the country's economy is driven by it. Without water, the crops have failed. Between the drought and the war, thousands and thousands of Somali people have lost everything. Mogadishu, the country's capital, has been especially affected.

Despite its difficult history, Somalia has a long oral tradition and is known as a nation of poets. K'naan grew up in that tradition at the knee of his famous grandfather. We are fortunate that he was able to move to North America and share his poems and songs with the world.

Photo credit: Patrick Hoelek

K'NAAN is a singer and poet. He is best known for his song "Wavin' Flag," which carries an important message of hope.

K'naan was born in a part of Africa called Somalia. This book is about the beautiful country K'naan came from and the strong people who live there.

When K'naan was thirteen, war broke out in Somalia and he had to leave. With his mother, brother, and sister, K'naan came to North America as a refugee, looking for a more peaceful life. K'naan's family settled in Toronto, where he went to school and struggled to fit into a new culture and speak a new language. It wasn't easy, but he succeeded!

K'naan has used his interest in words and music to build a life doing what he loves most – singing and creating poetry. Some of his songs are about difficult issues, but K'naan writes them to show the power that each and every one of us has to improve our lives.

From his home in New York, K'naan continues to make music and work with people and organizations in Somalia. He wants to help create a safer and easier country for them. K'naan believes that everyone can make their dreams come true. He wants children to fill their lives with hope, and to think about how to make the lives of other people in the world better too.

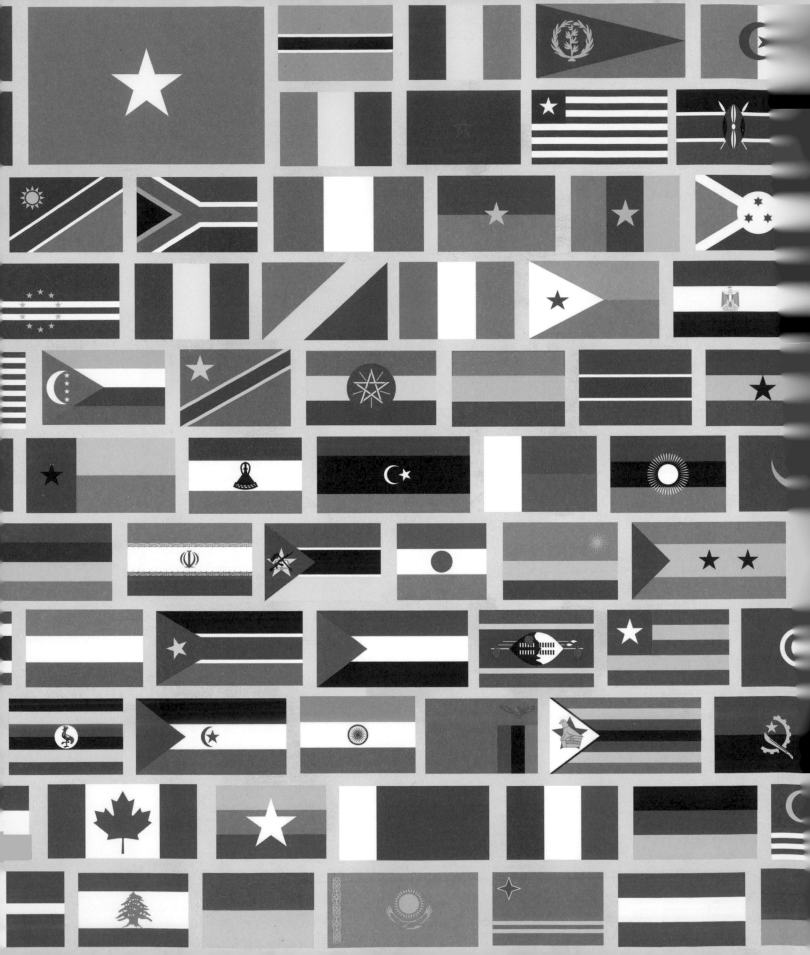